My first thought when I wake.

YOU MAKE ME

COMPLETE.

Just Married

You are everything.

You are the sun.

You are my fire.

Boundless love.

LET'S EXPLORE LIFE TOGETHER.

YOU ARE
THE ONLY STAR
IN THE SKY.

YOUR VOICE IS MUSIC TO MY EARS.

All of life's paths have led me to you.

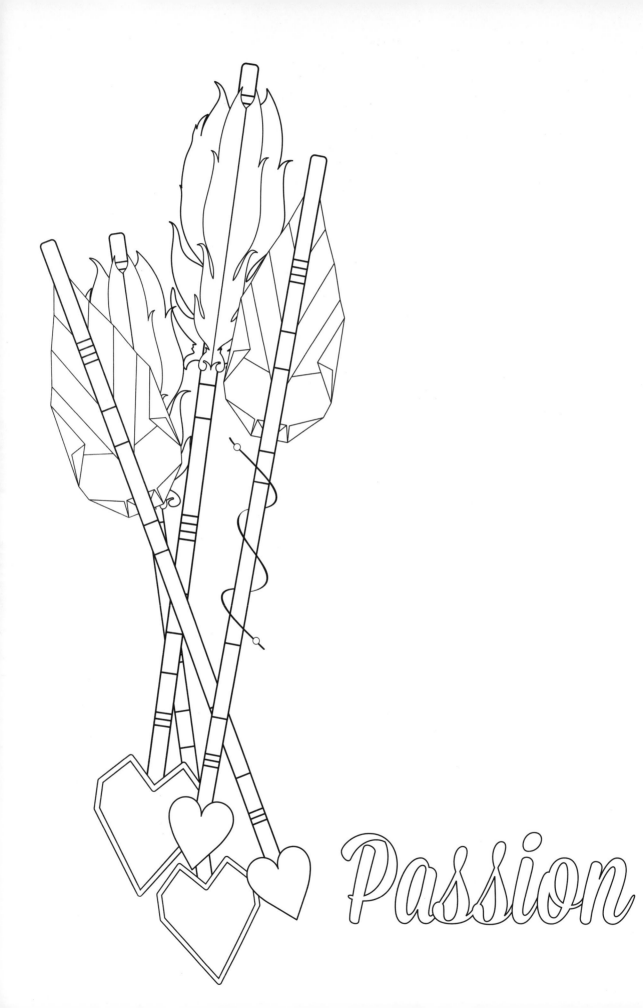

Passion

A flower that blooms only for me.

Your heart is my home.

You are my destination.

You nourish my soul.

You quench my thirst.

You are essential to me.

You ♥ ARE the best THING that EVER HAPPENED to me. ♥

You are my heartbeat.

Mine, forever.

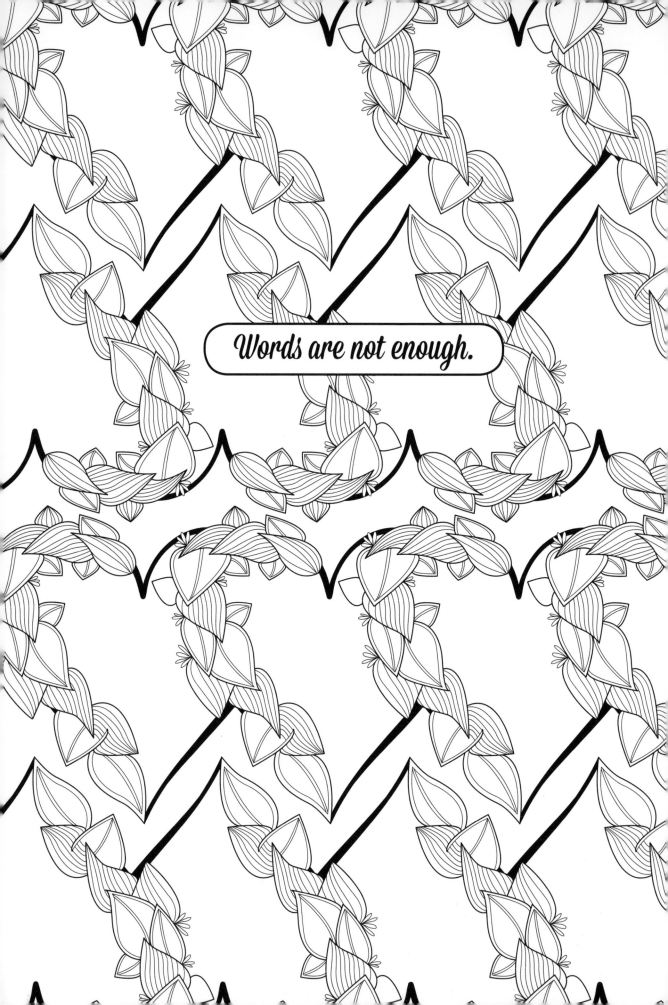

Words are not enough.

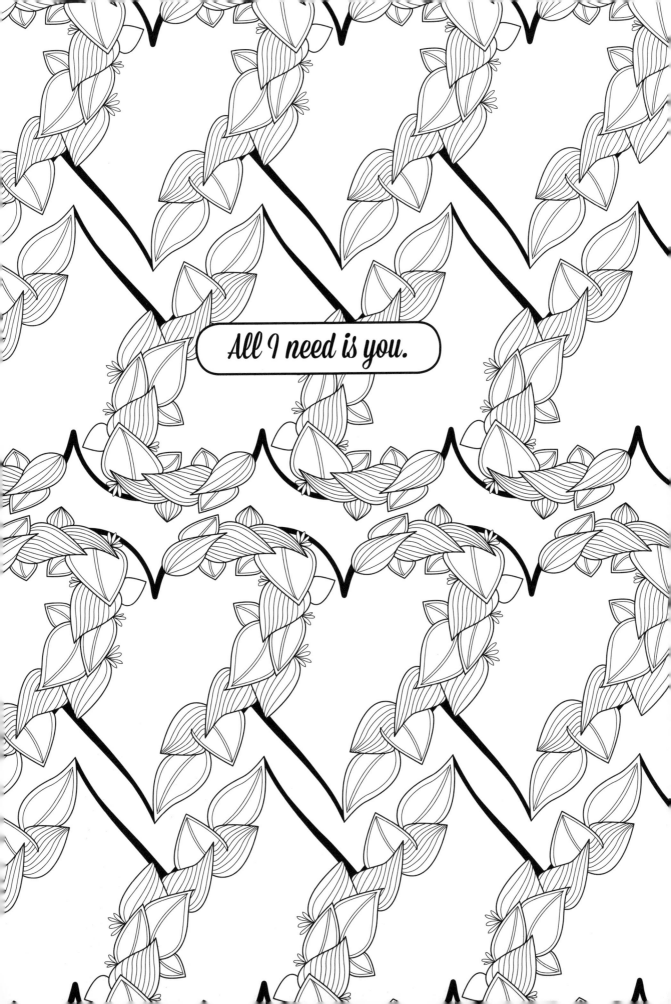

All I need is you.

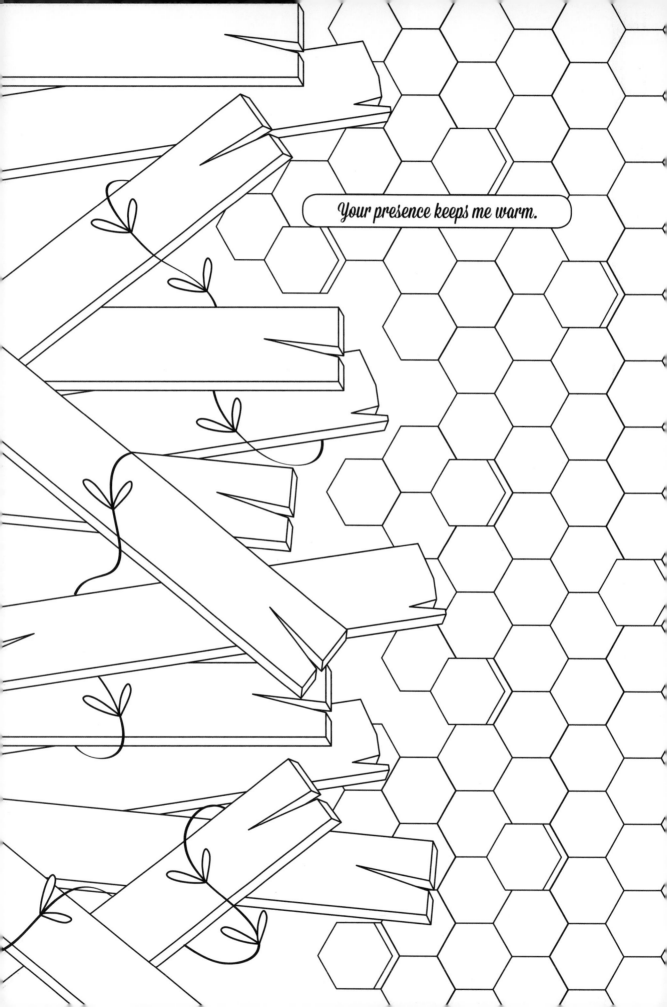

You embody all that is good in the world.

You are in my dreams.

Always by my side.

No star shines brighter.

Your smile lights up my day.

There is only us.

YOU ARE MORE THAN I DARED TO DREAM.

I DAYDREAM ABOUT YOU WHEN WE ARE APART.

AT
THE END
OF THE DAY...

Infinite love.

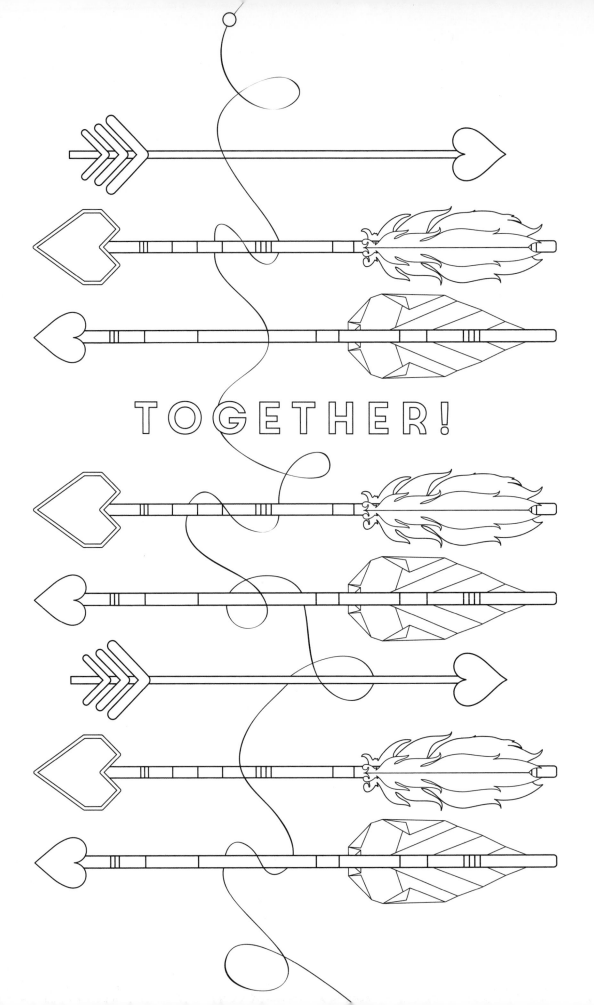

TOGETHER!

My constant companion.

ANI OHEV OTCHA

SZERETLEK

Taim i' ngra leat

Ti amo

Es tevi Milu

AS TAVE MYLIU

ECH HUN DESCH GAER

Ta sakam

Jeg elsker deg

Kocham Cie

TE IU BESC

TE AMO

JA ALSKAR DIG

Ti tengu cara

I love you

Seni Seviyorum

MILUJI TE

JE T'AIME

Ich liebe Dich

S'agapo

Mina rakastan sinua

YES KEZI SEEROOM YEM

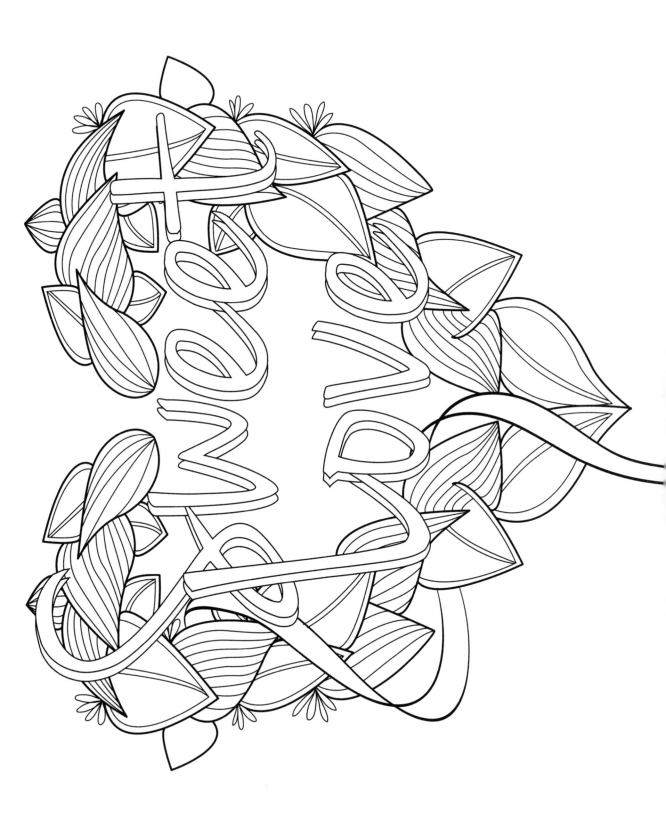

You are in every breath I take.

I cannot imagine being without you.

I give you all that I have.

Share everything.

YOU HOLD THE KEY
TO MY **HEART**.

You are mine,

I am yours.

MY HEART IS
IN YOUR HANDS.

Your love is the greatest gift.

You are my good-luck charm.

The sweet
fragrance of you.

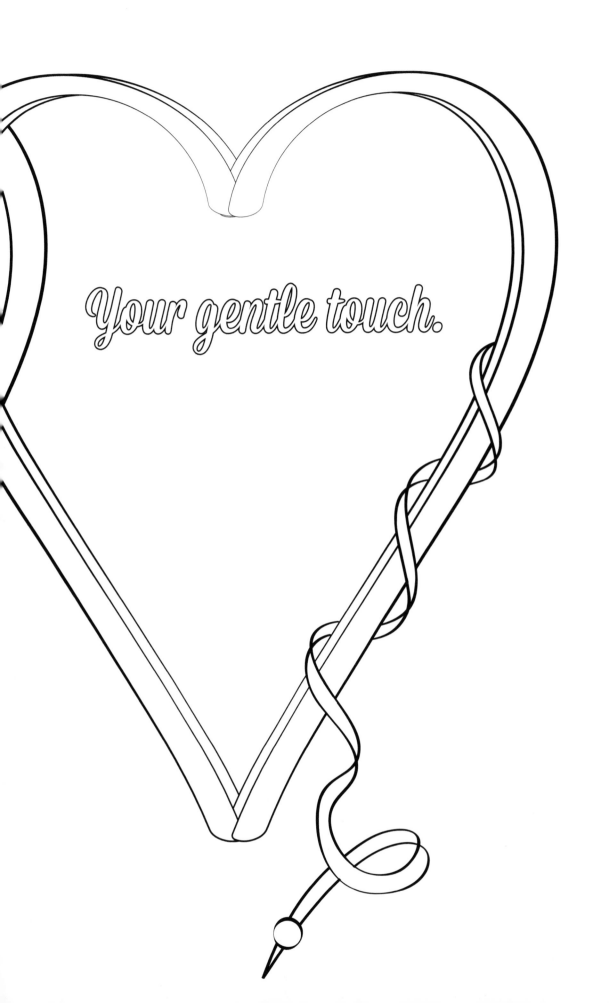

Your gentle touch.

You make life sweeter.

You light up
the room.

Love is timeless.

I am always here

for you.

Nature's beauty.

I was waiting for you.

You are the definition of love.

Love does not judge.

I love you
just as you are.

I love
every inch of you.

I cherish EVERY kiss.

I love everything you do.

I need your touch.

Storybook love.

EVERYTHING

I **NEED**

IS IN **YOU.**

Every
MOMENT
with you
is precious.

YOU BRING
A SMILE
TO
MY FACE.

SIT
WITH ME
IN SILENCE
AND
IN LOVE.

Because it's you .

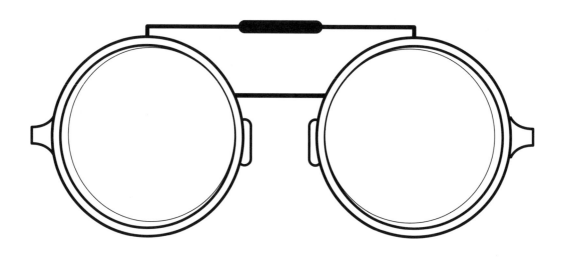

Because it's me .

You paint my life with every COLOR.

The day we met.

The moment I knew.

My darling.

Love knows no limits.

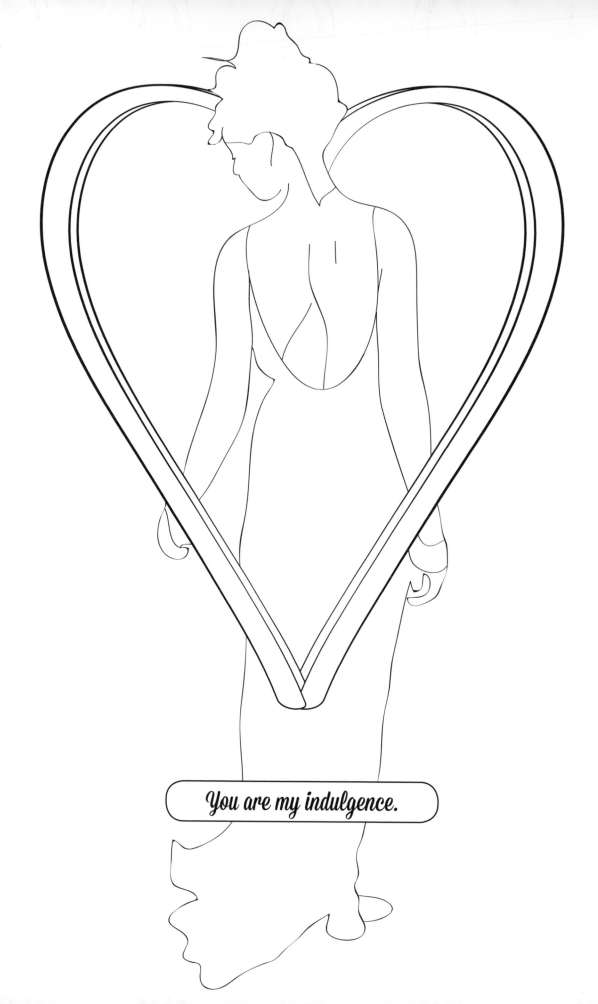

You are my indulgence.

Connection

This is how

I express

MY LOVE.

Happiness is being with you.

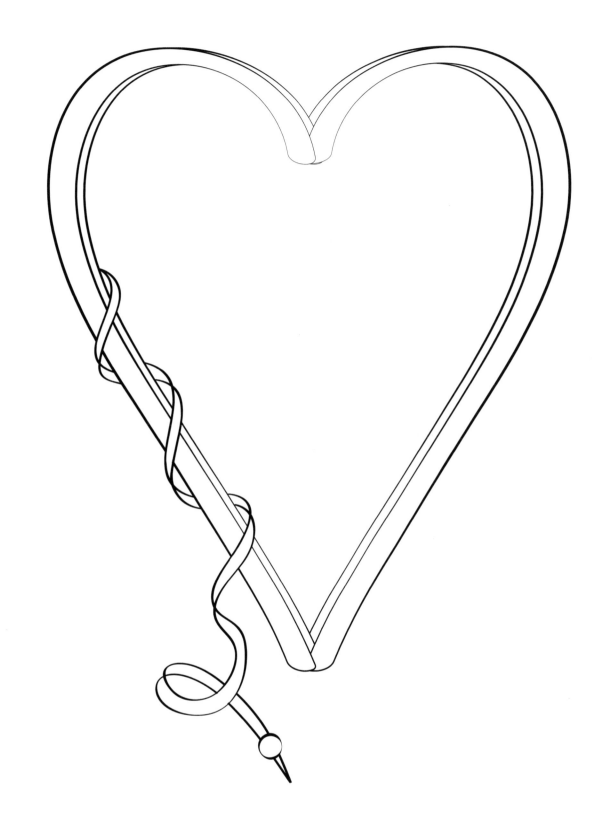

With your love, I can do anything.

There when I need you.

You're the artist!